Violeta Orozco's *Atlas of an Ancient World* has a foot planted within the many ecosystems of the Earth, allowing the reader to travel up to towering volcanoes and back down to spongy marshes to connect with the most vulnerable crustaceans. It has its other foot in the netherworld, a world of tías who appear, disappear, and reappear again, where ancestors "trade tales like beads" and offer wisdom we may have forgotten. Key sites in Mexico and throughout the Americas inform the reader of the valuable lessons rooted in environment and mythology. Dismembered goddesses are reminders of the strength of women who resurface from the dirt and remind us of our legends. Despite syntax that reads like an environmental study, you'll find the author admits to a love of the urban scent of oil, complicating our notion of the natural, even devoting a contrapuntal to the Jersey Shore. Prepare to travel with a magnifying glass that amplifies the forgotten, the disappeared, the microscopic, the ephemeral, all with a language that is lush and complex, using English, Spanish, and Nahuatl seamlessly. Orozco's work is a triumph which resonates and will beckon you to return, and return, and return.

—Dr. Grisel Y. Acosta

Young poets emerge timelessly and continually, if we nurture their ground with care and attention. Violeta Orozco's *Atlas of an Ancient World* reminds her readers of this necessity and truth. Her brave revealing of her heritage and homeland forces us in a gentle way, to "think about the soil, about your home," that history matters. She opens our eyes to the landscape of her people and her ability to continue on with her own journey. "I seek permission to enter this land." Welcome the heartache this provocative collection delivers. Walk with her, she is teaching us all.

—Louise Waakaa'igan

www.blacklawrence.com

Executive Editor: Diane Goettel
Cover Design: Zoe Norvell
Cover Art: "La barca de los sueños" by Perla Temoltzin
Book Design: Amy Freels

In June of 2023, Black Lawrence Press welcomed numerous existing and forthcoming Nomadic Press titles to our catalogue. The book that you hold in your hands is one of the forthcoming Nomadic Press titles that we acquired.

Published 2024 by Black Lawrence Press.
Printed in the United States.

ATLAS OF AN
ANCIENT WORLD

VIOLETA OROZCO

To my mother, whose ancestral understanding of her artistic craft as a sculptor paved the way for the spiritual relationship I bear to poetry today. With deep admiration for your wisdom and true knowledge of who we have always been as a people.

CONTENTS

Part 3. Urban Borderlands

PART 1. DREAMSONGS

ATLAS OF AN ANCIENT WORLD

A former library book made its way into my hands
like a shoaled fish all the way from Lubbock, Texas
the word "Discard" branded upon its back,
ink seared into the flesh of each page.

It was called *Peoples and Places of the Past*
as if it had been written in a perpetual present
that could never see itself with marveled eyes,

a book so unwieldy I had to use a horse
to carry it home, turn the first page,
let history unfold in tales of gypsum caves and Anasazi pottery,
desert towns in Paquimé, lake villages of adobe and stone.

How many years did the book spend
lying upon the patient shelves of the public library?
waiting for a shy reader to wander into its pages
admiring the eons it took to be formed
like a sedimentary stone

gathering geological memories of the earth

all the way to this era of human writing.

For how long, so many of us were waiting

for those words, climbing down dead craters

to read the injured surface of the planet.

It was rumored that once the book was reopened,

the sacred bison would repopulate the land

if rubbed with the right ointment on the paper.

No longer living in a cloistered world

    obsidian traders and cockleshell hunters

    decided to remove their knowledge

from the stone slabs of the ancient canyon.

Let them figure it out themselves

the wise women said, rowing away

from the islands, *we will keep our oracle*

for our private use. Why should we sell what we still need?

They took their dead with them

Stowed corn and wild rice in rafts

settled the other half of the world

one where no grains or crops would prosper.

They refused nostalgia, dwellings for the departed.

The word came across early enough

etched in the back of a condor:

empires had spent too much time

worshiping death,

they had lost the connection

to their celestial power,

ceased to nourish themselves with flowers and cacti

learn from the heart of plants

listen to the throb of woodlands and deserts

highlands and far away coasts.

This is the story of their story.

Let us trade tales like beads, and listen.

TLACUILA AT SERPENT MOUND

For many years I was afraid of the language of seers and curanderas,
           so akin did it seem to the language of death.
I did not want to be the dream-gazer, uttering auguries like nightmares
           stories of dismembered deer dripping into the sky,
           forming The Constellation of Quetzalcóatl,
           feathered serpent   cunning astronomer,
           looter of ancestor bones in a jade bowl.

I was only a Tlacuila, a humble female painter transcribing
           oak moans and rumbles in the deep forests of the mind.
I never saw myself as harbinger of hope or faith
           not having grown in a world of saints but of spirits
           dwelling inside mountains and oceans,

my language the murmur of creeks and winds beating
           upon the highest peaks. When I reached Serpent Mound I did
             not see
           the former denizens of this Ohio land. They were silent

like dead scattered barns splayed in a midwestern town

      where "effigy mound", "geoglyphs", and "ceremonial grounds"

      were nothing but feeble signs trying to explain to the white gaze

      why they should drive this far, how this burial site

      was still full of life and memory

      even after the Adena or the Hopewell disappeared.

They, who like the serpent-loving people of Aztlán,

      traded obsidian blades for turquoise

      bird-shaped pendants,

      imported grizzly bear teeth from the Rockies,

      carved shell beads from Florida to adorn the neck of the buried.

Across valleys and hills, they hammered copper into falcons,

      thin mica sheets from the Appalachian Mountains

      into undulating serpents and hawk talons.

This was no ossuary or graveyard,

      but a dream-vessel sheltering the last of their buildings,

      earthworks of a forgotten architecture

Enduring

everything infused with movement

      Snake

      Sycamore

      Stream

           down the trail

slither swiftly

    whirl

      into the coil of time

   eagle-traced map of dreams

   path of swallowed stars

where silver

      maples gaze down

at the pulsing water.

VOLCÁN DEL XITLE

Who is my inheritance now?

I look out at the vast serene black rocks
unfolding in space like hot magma.

They have been cool for centuries now,
lie like peaceful coals surrounded by a vastness

so green only the sea can sway like this deep forest
moving at the same pace of my thoughts now subdued

to hold only the grace of this silence
the graceful gravity of this silence.

For decades I have been terrified of silence.
It has eaten me up slowly and evenly

until I have stopped knowing how to speak
any form of truth akin to mine.

Who am I to echo in this might?

It is different this time,

this crater has given me a size, a dimension

eclipsing my own darkness,

any reason I have ever come up with to withhold

the true origins of my dark matter

traveling through uneven empires of dim sky.

All along I was reading the wrong signs

taking nightmares for omens, fireflies for fires,

in a forest that was never meant as a menace.

Mother, please forgive my blindness.

I cannot even read my own dreams,

quell your sobs when sudden lava flows

flood in like afterlives of cities we never did inhabit.

I don't know why I end here, thinking about you,

and the trees we both loved without knowing

they had a shape we both recognized

as our own, the weeping leaves of the sturdiest tree

holding the weight as we climbed

the pirul canopy, a thick shield of leaves shading us

from the terrible ogling of the world.

Now I know

that whatever I mistook for fragility

was made of the same solid basalt

I am standing upon.

This is my inheritance,

este volcán   flowing like a starlit stream

rushing into the human sky.

MOUNTAIN DAHLIA / EL PIRUL

*In memory of the mountain in Lomas Verdes where I
used to play as a child, now replaced by a large mall.*

Shielded under the memory

    of the longest brevity we may ever be

        we will dream clearer sources

gather

    rainwater to pour into the dam

        so when they slaughter this hill

some may remain

    folded in the flowers

        straw dahlias

growing on the edge of every mountain sensing death

    they will wave pink heads,

        sway long stalks into the air.

If we are brief enough to remember every tree

    leaves will hold the memory of our sight

        rebuild themselves after they have left our mind

California pepper trees still will send seeds

    years after they have been cut down.

Howling winds will feel the emptiness of skies

    that have lived a long time with mountains.

By then we will have taken

    the fifteen species of cacti into our hands

        cradled their delicate thorns in our raw skin

their displaced bodies will take over our gardens

    bringing back butterflies and crickets who fled

        this crumbling patch of land

  knowing

    this brevity

        still carries

scent of pink peppercorns from a native tree:

    el pirul

        a burning pungence

    traveling

        through these warm hands.

DREAMTIME / WOMAN HOLDING ATLATL

Lightning woman streaks angry stars across the sky.

Who can see her armed

silhouette walking through the night?

Glittering jade and malachite

flash like fireflies, deck caverns

long hidden from human sight,

tree rings count

floating whorls of liquid time.

Cave paintings show spears

piercing a tree's heart, billowing clouds

protect the rain she grows

with lightning bolts

even now that her ancestors buried

her blunt machete into the dry earth.

Under naked dawn light shining on woven tapestries,
women in outdoor markets trade coyote furs,
visions overlap in celestial mountain kingdoms.
A fox cuts loose from the painting, unfolds limbs,
leaps into a third dimension untouched.

He lands inside our world where we may kill
whatever we fear or dream to be too close.

How to return to that dreamworld?
where songs like talismans are worn
without shivering, proudly around our throat,
where hail and lightning
are hurled by a woman etched into stars
hollering into the closing threshold of the hours
thundering worlds too deaf to see her shaft
too blind to ask who the hailbearer may be,
how she cleaves screech from dream,
constellation from dreamtime.

LA FLOR DE CALABAZA

Think about the soil,
     about your home,
          the rhizome spiraling
through the underground
passages of water
     and earth tunneling
     into the realms
          of nocturnal sunlight.

And how will these buds ever bloom?
What faith keeps them glued
to their imaginary growth?
     How will they burst
     forth from the cocoon of spring?
          Interweave with other roots
          that climb and tangle
               until they reach
          the crust of the earth
               the frond
          climbing up the fence like an infinite beanstalk

The campesino's hands

counting

      the pepitas

he'll place in every hole,

      Building a mighty trellis

to arch the backbone

      of the creeping tendril.

How could this vine

      tower

above the lowly earth

      shoot

above the arrogant steeple

      crowd the whole

garden like a wiry weed

that once fed

a todo un continente?

I have watched this stalk rush

      skyward

like a green tendril

reaching toward

                    the ladder

            that thrusts

            its rungs into the clouds

            intertwining

                    La tierra

                            Y el cielo.

            I have entered

        the jicara's heart.

        I have drunk

        water from the ever-

        replenishing well,

                    the gourd that guards

                            the water.

        I have been fed

        by these yellow flowers

        night and day,

                    this pumpkin pulp

                    has sweetened my hunger

                    for centuries now,

the roasted green seeds

passed on from generation

to generation. Our hands a hot comal

where las semillas de la calabaza

grow hot and jump up,

        away into the wind who scattered them far,

            far from the ground who swaddled their

              sprouts

                curled their green embroidery

                  into that other field we call

                  the sky.

LOS VOLADORES DE PAPANTLA

Watch the twirling dance of flight,
the undying spiral of ascending men
the tapping of the shoes upon the drum.
30 meters high above the ground
danzantes unravel from a giant pole
follow the steady beat of the flute,
sound tangles like a vine onto the air.

If they would take off the strings
that held them to the pole,
they would still circle
the invisible axis of the sky
as if a giant tree
had been planted
at the center of the world
unmovable and strong,
centuries before any aircraft could deliver
a fragile body
safely to the ground,

Los voladores de Papantla

perch at the top of the old world

look down at the naive new tourists recording

the feat of a people

they never understood,

their panting cameras

click furiously away

at the human birds

who played their songs

atop their man-made trees

remembering

their joyous proximity to the ancient skies.

DESERT SENTINELS / SABINO CANYON

"Beware of Dog" the first sign seen

from a road's edge gleams.

Sun grazes

the thorny forehead of the cactus.

Everyone knows

who the real guardian of the house is,

backyard lined with green-armed guards

standing as tall as the mountains in the background.

Sentinels of stone and sand,

the Santa Catalina mountains

wait in their scorched silence

unfettering multitudes into the Sabino Canyon.

This
is our rocky home

this strip of jolted earth
creased into golden folds of rock,

this is the dream-drenched beam
of the Sonoran range.

Meet mesquite and saguaro, greet them
as you'd salute one revered by time and wind

resizing moons and open skies
jutting into the rocky craters of the earth.

They tell time in tides
and crushed spines,

blackened backbones, tree-rings
upon a desert's dry shores.

The cactus carcass marks time

inside her body, saving water

and monsoon sights for seasons

emptied of blue fields

when the hot stare of the red stain

sets fire to the Tucson mountains.

EL TECOLOTE

I. Barred Owl Alights in Snow

I felt the muffled flutter of a wingspan swirl

before I saw him plunge, a spotted blanket of stars

hovering high above the ravine of time

white-flecked twigs whisper

as they see the barred owl

glide into the snowy arms of the forest.

I awaken.

As if I had never been alive,

the mouse in me stirs as I look up   dazed

my body knows where he perched

better than my eyes   scanning tree rows

before the sunset holds its dim torch close.

All the dark rooms

in which a body could be placed

to sense the warmth of living hands

come to mind as I seek him

feathers transfigured into coarser bark,

wood-carved effigy returning to the stillness you have known.

Four times I tiptoed to the bottom of his tree.

Four times he left his perch among hickory and ash

skirted paths of cardinals and crows in maple groves.

He circled away,

the forest a crystal box where every sound was held

by the deep memory of the snow.

II. Tecolote as Shapeshifter

Shapeshifter who comes to me at dusk

catching the sunset in the clasp of your talons,

swiftly deliver the message you may carry.

What fruit do the boughs of my destiny yield?

I feel your gaze as one feels the weight

of human eyes

unshielded to arrows piercing layers of cloud and canopy

fastening your vision on my wingless body

as I slither like a reptile among the low leaves,

scamper blindly across the trembling branches

fearing the invisible forces of winter skies bringing down

the lightning bird, the feather-storm.

Oh, shapeshifter, dusk-spirit, two-faced nahual,

. Tecolote I never hoped to find in this snow-realm

I seek permission to enter this land

 you command and surveil.

Oh, carrier of ancient news,

what tidings do you bring from the other side?

Our eyes have met at last,
among snow flurries like soft words

exchanged on a cold night.
I sense you as you sense me

walk
slowly toward your tree

in the gasping silence of this sphere
where the flakes numbly fall

and gather in the forest ground.
I lose you. Before we can even talk,

old soulmates whispering and hushing
at the slightest crackle of the rustling branch.

Only the wind knows where you have flown.
I watch your great wingspan swell, circle treetops

like a mother brushing the soft head of her child.
Swoosh away, dark keeper of my fate,

sweep the fir tree clear of any blight.

I trust you will land safely

in hushed realms of brown dreams

the color of your plumage

where we may meet once I receive   from you

the fleeting gift of flight.

CLIFF DIVERS / LOS CLAVADISTAS

Fuel is my hands
    recharged by wet, cold sand,
    beach bonfires at the Pacific shore
        making white crabs shimmer, lit-up ghosts
            flickering under dark-
            pitched waves

tropical summer storms taunt lightning
    dip our electric bodies
    into shimmering water

the thrill of the forbidden arts
    of chasing death
    has the panting taste of life
        as you scuttle across wet cliffs
        nimble crustacean born to roam salty boulders
jagged bluffs that roar and puff in the thrashing water
    while we look down from the headland
    arms outstretched toward the foam

we pretended we would throw

      each other into the black sharp crags

      of La Punta Negra

      ocean infested with aguamalas and stingrays

you dreamed you would become a diver as brave

as those you saw jump off La Quebrada

      the great Acapulco gulch

      where sheer cliff walls

            gape at your soft breakable body

            preparing itself for flight

churning waves wait

      like patient sharks

      for the signal of the first blood-

      curdling whistle of the race

            the narrow space between rock walls

            closes in on you

the surge of the water

rises to meet you in midair

      you somersault into the sky like a swallow

      chest puffed out, arms outstretched, head held high

your torso a blur of rock-colored limbs

      plunges as the sun sinks its last rays

            into the edge of the coast

blue-white currents

      sizzle between the rocks

      a turquoise rampage

            where four children play

            with the wild forces of the earth

their joy is invisible fuel shooting

      from their young arms, a lungful of laughter

      encompassing

            the grace of the very first leap

            of the child into the planet

                  a fish out of water

                  eyes closed to withstand

                        the full force of the atmosphere

                        rush into his bloodstream

                            like a newfound planet

                            streaming into our open pores.

HOW I CONTRIBUTED TO THE
DESTRUCTION OF MARINE ECOSYSTEMS

Through my window

I watched a mother's hand

steady her child as she

>   balanced on the edge of the sidewalk

>   as if she too had been trained in teetering.

Two times ten the wobbling girl traveled me in time,

>   my naked toes shifted their weight between

>   wet barnacle-covered rocks on a rugged shoreline.

A single false step might have harpooned my spine

>   my head—a brittle shell—hovered above the surf.

>   I trusted the sea would not betray me.

>   The coral reef knew me as well as I knew her.

>   So often I had tributed my blood

>   to the reef's rocks, stung by sea urchins,

thick thorns thrusting living spears into my skin,

A central part of the reefing ritual

      skin schooled by jellyfish

      electric tentacles tangling their wires

      into my nerves, the ocean a network

           of connecting cables

anemones dangling tentacles

my fingers making contact

           like an astronaut hesitant to leave her suit.

      A naked mollusk,

I bared my unshelled body to the water

      skirted stingrays

      flaming fire corals, fierce puffer fish.

I knew

      I was not supposed to touch,

but a nude hermit crab

      came out of my own shell

      crawled among rocks

      to find a new home for her growing body,

           shed fear of predators only for an instant

              pincers turned to fingers

prodded the seabed, feelers and eyes groped

the direction of the ocean currents,

gripped the edge of a changing shoreline

where corals crumbled

at a child's touch

the whole reef reeling like a

single body

suspended between

earth and water.

LA MULATA DE CÓRDOBA

The folk tale

Five hundred years ago
a black ancestor clutched

the bars of a prison at a colonial Mexican fort
sentenced to death for refusing to fuck

the white mayor of the city of Córdoba
for as long as he liked

how dare she refuse his hand
a woman named loneliness

Yet he was afraid of Soledad's revenge
called her Black sorceress

Aliada del diablo
Bruja de San Juan de Ulúa

La Mulata de Córdoba
was said to freeze the gaze of a young man

doomed to wane until death bore him away
her special herbs would cure

the ailing health of women
and make unloving men

swoon under her spells
love potions and bountiful gold coins

flowed from her robes
into the hands of the wretched and poor

The holy inquisition had her locked
up in the Spanish fort in Veracruz

until she found
a piece of charcoal

She traced
the outline of a ship on her stone cell wall

a black freighter
with billowed sails

(A sailor saw her once aboard a pirate ship
her gold hoop earrings

flashing
in the pitch-black night)

Legend has it
one rainy evening

at The Gulf of Mexico's gray shores
on the eve of the day

she'd be let out to be burned
her drawing was completed, so perfect every spar

and rope were standing
as if waiting for the wind

the guard stared at the drawing
sensing something wrong

he caught the threatening mast
starting to move

out of the corner of his eye
the enormous beam

towered above him
a charcoal drawing so alive

La Mulata asked *What else do you think it needs*
to come to life?

Only to sail the jail guard said, and with those words
storm gusts began to blow

she broke into a laugh and waved goodbye
before she jumped into the deck

the ship sailed away in a dark storm
while the guard was left clutching

at a charcoal painting
sketched upon an empty prison cell.

PART 2. TALISMANS FOR THE DISPERSED

WRITTEN AFTER A PHOTOGRAPH FOUND IN MY FATHER'S BASEMENT

My country frozen in time

two years before the earthquake

I didn't get to experience,

molcajete on the cupboard

right about to fall

off the spice cabinet

dangerously teetering on the edge.

My mother's dark hair

let loose to set fire

to the whole kitchen,

her laughter

lighting up the photograph.

I can't quite place the date.

We all look young in the eyes of the beloved.

I can't see my brother's face.

Only the back of his head,

his light hair crisscrossed by the sun.

He's facing me in the picture,

I wonder what he said to make me smile.

A shiver runs down my spine as I realize

I don't know who took that photograph.

No one outside the picture knows

or remembers

who was behind the lens that day,

capturing every ray that filtered through a door

no longer there.

My father looks intently at his breakfast

of quesadilla de flor de calabaza, some quiet joy

is making his face glow, unaware

of how close we were to dispersion,

the solid oak table congregating us

to the ritual of daily sustenance,

my mother's voice

calling out to us from the kitchen,

reaching into the farthest

crevasses of the house

crossing

through long tunnels of time

pulling us together across space

toward the only moment

we would ever share

over and over again,

engraving memory into the skull

developing the invisible film

of history.

A RED CANNONDALE LOST IN HOMER, ALASKA, CIRCA 1980

The bicycle he bought in Alaska
reappeared in central Mexico
forty years after he had sold it
to a Korean fisherman
who worked in the king crab industry.

It was the same 1980's make, had the same dent
he made as he rode through miles of fjords
in the short summer at the edge of the Arctic.

His disbelief made his bike disappear
as the cherished things in dreams
slip away even as we stare
intently at them, trying to hold
them steadfast in our gaze
pin them down to the present,

refusing the transformation of all things brittle

our desperate hands clawing at the waterfall

bicycles morphing into bats flying out of frozen caves

or crevasses so deep the bottom

lies nowhere in sight.

Within that watery world

few things ring true:

the key we lost, the queen of Spring's fair face

glimmering past the clutch

of her mother's arms, her wail

for the girl torn from her womb,

Xochiquetzal swiftly swallowed by the greedy earth

her underground journey away from the light

flowers shriveling into eleven months of darkness

out of the realm of all things reachable

standing in the gateway that divides

desire from dream

dream from vision

bicycle from owner,

my father's waning memory hailing back

to whatever shimmered as a familiar truth

in any land

summoning from afar.

EL ZAPATERO

The cobbler
that put soles in these boots
is dead.

A whole age
has gone by
after he left.

They don't fix shoes
in my old neighborhood
anymore.

I don't recognize
half the stores on this strip
once I returned.

They sprouted in the pandemic
like mushrooms after a storm.
This used to be my street

twenty years ago.

The cycle is complete.

I return

after nothing

here knows

where I came from.

LA APARECIDA

The neighbor told us
she came to say goodbye
twenty-five years later
she knocked on the same door
imagining someone
should be living there still.

But no one answered,
not even a dog
rushed out to meet her like before.

She might have come
six months ago, when he was still alive
and barking at every neighbor on the block.

What was she thinking?
Coming back like that into our lives,
when we'd already left for other cities,
my brother perched high
upon a steeple in Oaxaca,

restoring a 300-year-old dome,

his magic hands returning

baroque churches to their original aspect

while I gasped in awe at el milagro   the miracle

¡mi tía estaba viva!   my aunt was alive.

She was last seen on November first

Día de los Muertos niños

claiming she had come back:

La Desaparecida finalmente aparecida.

Strangest thing is my dad didn't see her.

He left the house to get milk and eggs,

milk and eggs for Christ's sake,

right at the same moment she walked

into her old haunts.

She never came back,

never left

a phone number,

an address

any sign or sound.

She left as she had come,

no warning or farewell.

I wonder what she had come to tell us,

even as I write

from another country,

my ear pressed to the ground

to catch the slightest beat

of her footsteps

upon my father's lawn.

LA DESAPARECIDA

She will leave her daughters behind her,
like a ship leaving behind a twin wake
      in an inhospitable ocean.

They will remember the laced green curtains hanging in the light,
like two lobes of watery joy lazily mirroring the garden she planted
      —a pendulum of abolished glass—
      while they played hide-and-seek
among the leaves of the ivy-covered wall, their mother's presence
a stalwart pine watching them from above.

She'd always bring them lunch at recess,
      her hands reaching through the bars
of the school with an avocado sandwich,
      always watching out for serpent signs
        of danger in the grass
          they played in,
            as tall as their growing bodies
          chasing each other behind classrooms

climbing the tallest trees to hide from the principal's frowns

their bodies bounding into the sun like two fawns

disappearing into the thicket.

Like their mother reabsorbed by time, her body leaping back

    untraceable

    their daily lunch supplanted

        with a bag of chips tossed into their backpack

            like a dead snake's rattle.

Father unable to make

        sense of who or where or what

        took her,

the table always bare,

cans like coffins sealed upon the shelves

dry tortillas and shriveled fruit

waiting

    on the kitchen counter.

THE TRUTHS WOMEN KNEW

After Anne Sexton's "The Truth the Dead Know"

Where is the space where your words will bloom?

instead of shriveling,

give rise to entire ecosystems,

woods with oaks and finches,

deserts birthing thirst

and shedding streams

after centuries of bounty.

You're tired of being quiet

of sitting still at school,

closing your legs and mouth

as if some deadly monster would emerge

from the muddy depths of your being.

The truths you knew would reach so far,

they would burn your mother's ears,

turn

your father's hair white

at the simple word *explain.*

Y por qué la tía Norma se tuvo que ir
to stay alive and sane,
her bruise-covered body
the only road she knew how to follow.

The battered tías left to swallow
their pride at their father's doorstep:
Regrésate con tu esposo
his words would never change,
even when omens and nightmares
surrounded
la vieja cabecera de su cama.

And how we would become the stories we fled from,
the ghosts we claimed not to believe in.

You felt condemned to predict death
by treason, cold-blooded plots
concocted by uncles
scheming to keep
the castle for themselves
release the spell of hatred
upon Rapunzel's land.

There was no kingdom to fight

for, only the greed

and strife among the families

murder by indifference,

words only murmured at hospitals

in deathbeds,

borracheras,

funerales.

You found such agony encased in words

that you grew afraid of speech,

would only write cartas

on a piece of paper

to get your messages across

the table,

when no one would listen

and no one dared speak.

You learned to speak in dreams

read tarot cards and cowries

puddles in the street after a storm.

Poems were nothing but another

mode of divination,

no more than coffee stains on a cup

behind the shelf,

waiting

for somebody to read them

somebody to hear

the truths

women in your family once knew.

FOLLOWING THE BIRDS

After W.S. Merwin's "Shore Birds"

Shall we follow the birds

    when they gather in

        turbulent flocks

            over the sun

How should we heed or hail

    the murmur in the bushes

        dark rumblings

            of a corvid tongue

Could we still speak

    to the screeching bramble

        as they roost like a black wig

            in a bald elm canopy

                settling like night

        upon a branch

    What do they talk about

the restless crows

as they shudder together

    like a sea-wave

        rippling

            into reddening skies

TIDAL BIRDS

It took me two years to learn to listen to the river.
She wasn't easy to fathom,
dark as she'd become after swarms of cities
settled upon her shores.

To her, every house was but a tiny dragonfly
shimmering a brief second in the sun.
She knew they would leave,
die off into the long summer.

She waited and listened like the cranes
patiently perched on the tidal river shoulder,
waiting for tides to ebb each month
so they could raid stream beds,
chase scuttling bugs.

Late afternoons would find them foraging for fish,
great blue herons emerged from the bushes,
armored guards flashed their silver sheen
at ebbing tides.

I almost learned their names,

predicted the place where they would land.

Caught in a circular net,

we chased each other before nightfall.

Snowy egrets line the estuary,

a ribbon of white foam across its flanks.

We stalk each other

watching out of the corner of our eye.

Nothing is ever still in this quiet marshland,

not even our bodies ambushing in stealth

while the frogs slide into the water

a pebble disturbing the watery surface of the sky.

DESERT NIGHT

Stars shy away from me as I
        drive away from you

sounds of the desert glide
        toward me in return

they mirror my silence
        as I think of you as the cacti

talk to each other in stillness
        in the moonlit canyon

uncovering round shapes
        below shimmering moonwater.

Amiga, no tienes que cuidarme.
I came to put my hand to the flames

reassign the seats of the dead and the living
shift the axis of the common stars.

THE THAWING

After Arthur Sze's "First Snow"

Absorb the weight of a pause

    when your foot falls soundless

        into a web of snow.

Follow feline tracks

    across man-made trail.

        Step out of the ditch,

it's getting dark and cold

    look down

        snow will turn to ice

push you toward the center

    a bug flailing on the edge

        of a steep bowl

slipping back

    toward grave

        grab   gravity

crater lake draws gulls

    to perch on frozen glass

        slopes of hills are thawing

beneath their webbed claws

    boy and girl follow

        into white field

brother loves to skate

    white pines motion

        from across the dam

PART 3. URBAN BORDERLANDS

THE CALL OF THE MOUNTAIN

Dedicado al Pico del Águila, Ciudad de México

The mountain is a treacherous site,
the son of an alpinist warned me.

Little did he know I had been raised
by an alpinist's son
in the mountains
of my native city.

Popocatépetl, Iztaccíhuatl,
Xinantécatl
Monte Tláloc
Cumbres del Ajusco.

The mountain will always try to kill you.

You must show her
the same respect
you show to the ocean.

The mountain will always cleanse your darkness.
The mountain is a lesson in humility.
Learn from your elders
or succumb to your own ignorance.

I learned from my elders
even when I became an elder
because I was treated
for so long as a child.

I learned from the mountain
even after I was long gone
from the volcanic cluster

Cuatzontle, Quepil, volcán pelado
al fondo los dos picachos
de San Miguel Ajusco

kept waving back to me, the lure
of the lava fields in Cañada limpia,
the cold sanctuary of stones.

Desde Malinalco hasta Las Cruces,

the people walked across the mountains

till they reached Chalma

La señora de las cuevas,

Ostotéotl

feminine aspect of Texcatlipoca.

They came across the firs and pines

to find a womb hidden

under a bleeding Christ.

Pinus jáuregui

Abies religiosa

bosque de oyameles

llévame a la diosa.

I will find

My own source of power in this mountain

I will hike the trails my elders once adored

The mountain bears the memories you forgot.

Serpientes de cascabel y talamontes

shake their rattle at me

while I climb

into the fanged sky,

El espinazo del diablo

gleams like a white fang atop a crowded city

3940 m above sea level

I tremble in the crevasse

carved between the peaks.

Pico del Águila

I have learned from death

even as a child

skirting a jagged precipice

howling above the treeline.

This is where I should stop.

But I never stopped.

I kept going,

even beyond the place

where the pines stopped growing.

Cruz del marqués.

Pino de altura.

Mujer de altura.

Because I lived in fear

most of my life,

I let my anger guide me

Every step toward the summit

decreased my fear

of being murdered, mugged, or raped

in my own city

by my own people.

Hija, la montaña es peligrosa.

But so was my city.

Nancy crashed into a semi.

Alex was run over by a bus.

Only now I am realizing

that it was always unrealistic to live.

I am indeed,

a true survivor

like these trees

holding their ground

in an encroaching city.

THE UNEARTHING OF THE COYOLXAUHQUI STONE

*Mexico City, 1978. Date of the discovery of La Diosa
under the ruins of the former city of Anáhuac*

When have I not been mourning,

when have I not sung low?

humming over cempazúchitl corpses

strewn on the pavement in the park.

My city

a carpet of petals,

trodden jacarandas in the spring.

Their purple hue sticks

to the darkest eye.

Color pulses through the arteries

of la plaza del Zócalo, Tenochtitlan,

Centro histórico de la Ciudad de México,

where Spaniards tore apart

the Aztec pyramid stone by stone

to build the cathedral with recycled bones

from the altars and Tzompantlis,

thinking we wouldn't find our way back to El Huey Teocalli

house of the former gods.

Let us mourn together for El Templo Mayor
found under the carcass of the church,
La Diosa torn limb to limb—
stripped naked upon a round stone slab
waiting more than four hundred years to be found.

La Coyolxauhqui, Aztec goddess of the moon,
still wore her plumed headdress, her warrior belt intact,
rattlesnake cascabeles still jangled from her cheeks
when unearthed by La compañía de Luz y Fuerza del Centro—
the puzzled electricians looking for a route
      to connect the frayed cables of the sinking city,
      the ancient lakebed quivering with the story of a girl
who dared defy her own mother.
All we know is first her brother chopped off her head,
      her body was thrown down the mountain,
         her limbs went their separate ways.

Her mother Coatlicue kept sweeping her temple,
      a baby in her belly getting ready to maim
      whoever threatened the body that fed him,
Lord Huitzilopochtli, el hombre de la casa,

he who battled the armies of the Southern Stars

            womb against womb

        Madre contra hija   tierra contra luna

        daughter against mother

brother against sister   sol contra luna

        todos contra una.

But that was not the war god's version of the facts.

Huitzilopochtli thought he was protecting his sacred right.

But he failed to notice que todas somos una.

Ahora nosotras somos Coyolxauhqui.

Somos las estrellas que no quisieron apagarse.

      We are the pulse,

we are the multitudes

marching toward a future

that cannot yet plumb

the depths of our strength,

our bodies breaking

into the hard pavement

emerging like roots

cracking

the stone sidewalk

that held us growing underneath the earth,

re-membering our constellation of scars.

Madre tierra

Madre Coatlicue

bring us back,

tráenos de vuelta.

Nosotras somos la luz, nosotras somos la fuerza.

THE METRO STRUGGLES

Weather advisory, snow in the Pacific Northwest,
every sinew tensed in the direction of tomorrow
or nunca   two women like poised arrows
wait for a standby flight in the December holidays.

My jaw tightens as I obsess over the flight
        I just missed. I wonder if she
                has come from as far as I, if she traversed
                thistle-covered cities and palaces of white marble hush
                ice-glazed bridges two rivers apart.

I stare at her, intrigued by jet black hair
        recalling all the buses and trains I'd barely boarded
        how my hands pried open metro doors in Ciudad de México,
        Mother of Millions, raced toward the closing doors of a car
        that threatened to leave the passengers behind every day,
the crowded metal animal swallowing bodies that hurled
themselves into the bursting subway,
        not a single spare seat for an extra soul at the rush hour,
        no room for one more needle in that haystack of a city,
and how against all odds, women managed to get in.

We squeezed ourselves between the negative space,

slick with rain from the five o›clock cloudburst,

    squirming between masculine

bodies that entrapped us

        a throbbing wall of sweaty skin—

     retractable flesh raised

        eagerly upward, ready to be thrust

        inside.

All the tricks I learned to stay safe in lusty mobs,

    stand my ground in raw male crowds,

      bite and claw to guard my place,

        I now aimed at one like myself.

      Our legs sprinted up escalators,

thrust themselves into concourses

    curse words clanging like swords and shields

    as I slid into the airplane gate.

Now that the battle for space reached us both,

pitted against two countries

        that lash out against us, unleashing

the sleeping volcano within

bringing out

the brunt   the burn   the power

to ignite

A COOLING BODY

Across this city's sky,

starlings zoom past

     taking the season away in their wings.

Early winter sweeps away any remains,

sudden gusts explode into the window

     shielding the living from the dead.

Only the morning frost

hangs like a hand of fog.

     Any city I have ever been in

carries the memory of my warm body,

one I cannot carry as I go

     losing heat into the atmosphere,

a star cooling down as it dies.

How many light years will it take

     to fall from the sky?

tearing down the fabric of the stellar tissue,

magnetic fields going haywire inside electric grids,

   city powering down like a nuclear plant,

gas and matter crashing like a grand piano

collapsing down the stairs, crushed skeleton

   disintegrating into the void.

Is this how cities end?

a general blackout where no sound ensues,

   no shock energy is released

to transition into another stage

the core of the world burnt out

   in less than a second.

JERSEY SHORE AS REPORTED BY A TRAIN PASSENGER

Eucalyptus, they grow anywhere

ask them how they flourish

in the gray industrial desert of New Jersey

where garbage under train tracks

blooms like an urban cactus

Remember those days as a brown haze

dead branches heaped below an underpass

bridges as far as the eye can see

as if earth was laid in layers

of endless roads, miles of expressways

snaking over rivers

starved against each other

bones rattling in empty sockets

Oil and waste ooze

black pus in bog meadows

reeds and roots poke out from shell middens

dissolved in brackish marshlands

crab cemeteries   unidentified tree corpse

lay between miles of suburban dread

rows amid rows of hunch-shaped houses

blurred trains gaze giddy visions of blind speed

smash buildings into each other in haste

to reach the shore   cleanse the vision

under so much blue

cobalt in the water

casting out its rays into the west

nets of hope

only the numb or despairing would jump

into the great waters of the East

thinking bodies freed from so much weight

lead in the current making way into the bloodstream

thirsty skin soaks up the sight

living shores unaware of trash tides

rise among grass dunes

inch their way along every grain of sand

forage for any sign of life

glisten like a metal rod

a conduit

connecting the veins of the land

to the still-beating heart of the ocean

NEW YEAR'S EVE IN SANTA CRUZ

In Remembrance of Gloria Anzaldua

Last day of the year and I've survived

      the growing familiarity with felled pines, mournful cypress trees

burnt tree-trunks on rock-studded coastlines.

For ten years I have been coming

      to this quiet garden

      where I mingle with oaks and hummingbirds

the lengthening steps to the lighthouse start to unburden their load.

No Christmas trees remain upon these cliffs

      the pelicans roost on polished crags, surveying blue,

I watch them unperch: stone unclasping cliff.

The bay calls out a soft, peeling sound

      draws the spinning world inward, waves whirling

toward the center of the water-shaped earth.

In the plum-colored house in the mountains someone sleeps

       at this very moment she may feel

someone is watching her. She sits up in bed

turn on a light, walk to the porch

       look out toward the Santa Cruz surf.

Only the splitting body of the waves

returns her intent gaze.

       How do you know that I am here?

I know you feel me, way beyond your death

as I feel you, blood within my bones

       surge as the swell heaves with foam

amada ancestra, hermana, guía.

FOR THOSE WHO THINK I BELONG TO MY COUNTRY

Every place i've been in
i'm counting down the seconds
      it takes me to split
      drop off a tree like a foreign apple
      five four three two
      bang bang i don't belong

The mailman asked my grandma
as he saw her clean her garden
if she could call
The Lady Of The House
La señora de la casa
      He thought there was no way
      a black woman in a country
      that refused to acknowledge its own blackness
      could be a queen

The teachers in La escuela primaria
Adolfo López Mateos

> told us there were no indios left
> that we were un país mestizo
> a successfully colonized country
> that Mexicans managed to kill them all
> kill the Indio in us
> refuse our own brown skin

My Father's kinky hair refused
to let his mother die in him
Her voice was strong
it sings through me
I
will never let her die
even if my skin
does not reflect her same hue

I will never let Her die

> ay ay ay Yemaya Oshún
> take me to the waters
> of the Mother Sea

AZCAPOTZALCO / ODE TO THE INDUSTRIAL PERIPHERIES OF MEXICO CITY

I never questioned
the origin of cats.

    I thought they sprang up like bacteria

    in a dying body

        like the myriads of factories

    erupting on every corner

    of Cuitláhuac, former Aztec stronghold

where armies of ants once swarmed into the city,

    train lines connected Azcapotzalco

    to Tlalnepantla's peripheries of dust.

This is how I was born. In this urban borderland

    where flower markets and corn fields

bloomed into refineries and warehouses almost

    overnight. Smells from the slaughterhouse

on my grandmother's block would drift

    to our noses on hot summer days, their squeals

a strident melody in the bustling morning.

I swear there were more cats than people in that house.

       My uncle had to buy a rifle just to get rid

of one of their nine lives for nine years

       until we took down that cat nest,

inside a pile of old rotten bricks,

       with a bulldozer.

Industrial soot and grime

       covered the food we ate

at the open-air market, El mercadito

       where fried fish communed

with salsa Valentina every Saturday.

I've never tasted tacos

       half as good as those,

the smoky flavor of the street

       mingled with motorbike roars

and car's exhaust pipes sputtering

       warm breath into my face.

My lungs grew up in smoke

       instead of air,

we all squinted

through a thick, gray film

    to see the Mexican mountains

of Iztaccíhuatl and Popocatépetl

    shrouded by a veil of smog.

Before I came to this midwestern woodland

    I didn't realize how much I missed

the smell

    of fossil fuels

burning

    like a bonfire

in the middle of the night.

STARGAZING IN THE OFFICE

After Norm Mattox's "Innerverse"

Radio telescopes listen to the galaxies

while I sit

    stuck

      in a revolving chair.

I spin around

like a sick satellite

    scintillating

      from nine to five.

I am stationary

but my eyes are full of stars.

    I turn my gaze inward

toward the screeching constellations

    of my cells

    no bronze bell will break

      the silvery face of this silence.

Alright. I will stop contemplating

the ceremonial dance,

      the horizontal breathing

           of nebulas and clouds.

But no light particles

will freeze the twilight spasm

      of the Hubble telescope's collapse.

      Others have travelled

these sky paths before,

           tried to find their way back

the silvery river like sturgeon

           swimming upstream in late May,

thousands at a time

           toward the source,

the churning waters a handful of stars

           dispersed among the eggs

the foam has left orbiting

           around the same pull

A million years ago.

ODE TO THE HILLY CITIES THAT KEPT ME FIT

Thank you, oh hill

for being there

while I was running late

for school or work

biking like a devil

to get rid of the extra minute

the extra mile

that kept me away from the place

where I ought to be on time.

I praise you, hills of Cincinnati

that have kept me lean

and supple

like a well-tuned violin.

If it weren't for you

I would be lazy and large

lumbering around in slow motion

walking on a flat earth

a flat city that did not challenge my strength

my limbs tired of sitting down

on an office chair all morning.

Praise to all the hilly

cities in the world

for they do not rely

on simple love

but on the hard love

of the people who have learned

to love the hills

their jagged scalps

in winter when the leaves

have left the stage

and all is left is a sharpness

challenged by a body

that is willing to go upward

against gravity

against time

ACKNOWLEDGMENTS

To the family of artists where I was fortunate enough to grow up in. My mother the sculptor, my brother the architect and my dad, the polyglot.

To my poetry workshop teachers of the English Department in the Creative Writing Program at University of Cincinnati, John Drury and Aditi Machado. With you I have learned the true rigor of traditional forms and have the chance to tame my pen into sonnets, ballads and mind-bending somersaults, even though none of them are here. To Rebecca Lindenberg, director of the Creative Writing program at the University of Cincinnati, whose forms of poetry class exposed me to more experimental forms of poetry and polishing syntax to the utmost degree.

To my workshop buddies at the University of Cincinnati's Creative Writing program, Rome Morgan, Holli Carrell, Paige Webb, Hassan Mirza, Andy Sia, Joly and my dear friend Hussain Ahmed whose extraordinary talent as a poet deeply connected with his spirituality has always been a guiding star.

To Poetas Chingonas writing workshop. Hermanas, you have workshopped so many of these poems with me. Thank you, Carla Schick, Susana Praver, Aideed Medina, Yaccaira Salvatierra, and Isa. I am honored to grow alongside you. You are my community on the East and West Coast.

To Círculo de Poetas and Writers and their annual conference, who made me part of the board and supported my literary work since 2020. Adela Najarro, Odilia Galván, Lucha Corpi, Paul Alponte and Javier Huerta, it has been wonderful working with you.

To the most supportive community of poets I have in Cincinnati, the Black and POC spoken artists, performers, and slam masters of Ohio. You have helped me perfect my stage craft and test myself in poetry slams across the Midwest. I will be forever grateful to Kimberley Bolden (Duwaup) and Moneeca Phillips for promoting my work and being a slam poetry judge and coach for Elementz and the Cincinnati high schools. Nate, Zeda, Janay, Sol, thank you all for performing with me in my second poetry book launch.

To Roya Marsh and Louise Waakigan and the amazing team of *Roots, Wounds, Words* in that wonderful performance workshop in NYC.

To Macondo Poetry workshop, who have supported my poetry and fiction for two years now.

To my boyfriend, who cooks whenever I have writing deadlines, which is all the time.

A special thanks to J.K. Fowler of Nomadic Press who accepted this manuscript for publication in Oakland, and to Diane Goettel and Black Lawrence Press who made that possible in New York.

POEMS PREVIOUSLY PUBLISHED IN LITERARY MAGAZINES

"How I Contributed to the Destruction of Marine Ecosystems"
Tuxedo Arts and Literature Journal

"La Mulata de Córdoba"
La libreta magazine

"La Desaparecida"
Gathering of the tribes magazine

"Jersey Shore as Reported by a Train Passenger"
Open Earth III. Eco Poems.

An internationally renowned Latina author from Mexico City, Violeta Orozco is a bilingual poet and fiction writer who has earned numerous accolades for her two poetry collections in English: *The Broken Woman Diaries*, published in Washington State by Andante Books 2022, winner of the Rising Stars Award at the International Latino Book Award; and *Stillness in the Land of Speed*, published by Jacar Press in 2023, winner of the New Voices Poetry Award and a Pushcart nomination. She has received an honorific mention by the Academy of American Poets, the Juan Felipe Herrera Gold Medal for the best book of poetry in English among other international literary prizes. She is currently completing her Ph.D. researching and translating Chicano and Latin American Literature, with a concentration in Creative Writing at University of Cincinnati. She is also the author of a book of essays in Spanish *Cómo recorrer una ciudad sin despertarla*, and the translator of *Dreaming With Mariposas* into Spanish.